THE WORLD'S U
GOLF JO

Remembered
by
Martin A. Ragaway

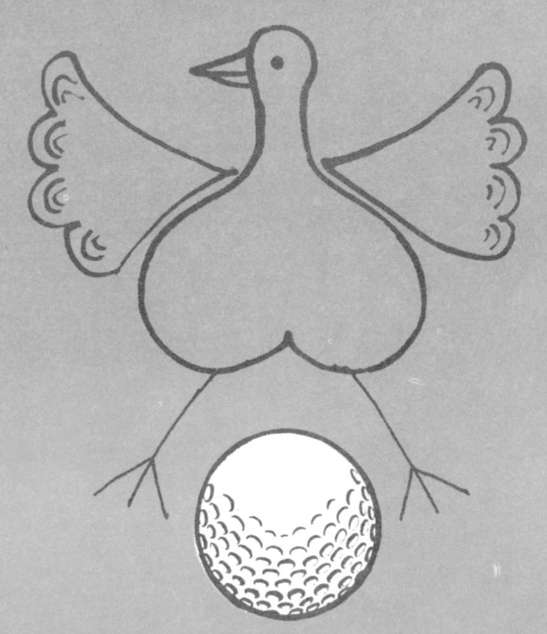

PRICE/STERN/SLOAN
Publishers, Inc., Los Angeles
1983

Golf is a game that steadies your nerves, toughens your muscles, improves your health and increases your stamina so you're strong enough to play again next week.

11th PRINTING – SEPTEMBER 1983

Published by Price/Stern/Sloan Publishers, Inc.
410 North La Cienega Boulevard, Los Angeles, California 90048

ISBN: 0-8431-0200-4

World's Worst Preface

Golf was invented in Scotland on October 3, 1106, at 11:15 in the morning. The very first golf joke was created at 1:30 the same afternoon. That joke appears in this book.

Golf was based on the old Roman game of Paganicus, which was played with a bent stick and a leather ball stuffed with feathers. The name was changed to Golf because most of the Pros refused to join anything called the Professional Paganicus Association.

In 1457, King James II banned "golfe" (as well as "futeball") because its popularity threatened the practice of archery for national defense. And even today, husbands still suffer the slings and arrows of wives who don't quite understand.

Incidentally, there are 10,000,000 golfers in the United States and only 9,999,999 balls in play. Which explains why at any given moment, somebody is looking for a lost ball.

Caddy, can you find balls in the rough?

Oh, yes sir ...

Good,
find one and we'll get started.

Your first day on the course?
How did you do?

I shot a 68– and tomorrow I
play the second hole.

Caddy, why do you keep looking at your watch?

It's not a watch, sir, it's a compass.

Please let me play through.

What's the rush, pal?

The battery on my golf cart is running down.

Golf sure is a stupid game.

You're absolutely right. I'm glad I don't have to play again until tomorrow.

Caddy, this is the toughest course I've ever played.

How can you tell, sir? You haven't been on it yet.

I gave up fishing for golf . . . and
I like golf much better.

Really, how come?

When you lie about golf, you don't
have to show anything.

Doctor: I'm afraid you're very run down. I suggest you lay off golf for a while and get a good day in at the office now and then.

Caddy, this is a water shot. Give me an old ball.

Begging your pardon, sir, but you've never had a ball long enough for it to get old.

You stupid idiot! You almost hit my wife with that ball!

I'm sorry, old chap. Here, take a shot at mine!

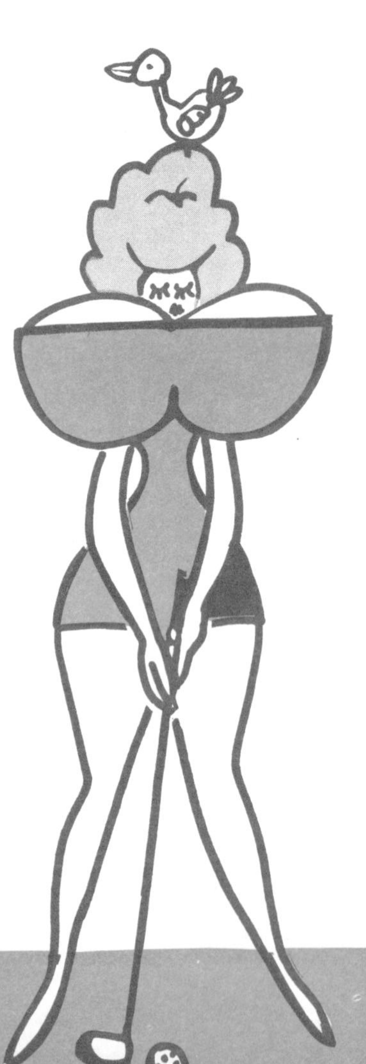

Lady golfer: What do you think of my equipment?

Man golfer: Great and I don't even know what you want to play!

First golf widow: Tell me, Helen, how do you get your husband to come to bed?

Second golf widow: Easy, I have a nightgown made of astroturf.

How does one meet
new people at this club?

Try picking up the wrong golf ball.

If I were you, I'd play golf for my health.

But I do play golf, doctor.

In that case, I'd quit.

One more bad shot will drive me crazy.

You don't need a drive - a short putt will do it.

I suppose you've seen worse golfers in your time . . . caddy, I said I suppose you've seen worse golfers in your time!

I heard you the first time, sir, I'm just trying to remember.

— Did you hear they've got a new formula that can grow hair on a golf ball?

— Great!

— Nah, it slows up the game too much!

— My doctor says I can't play golf.

— He saw you at the office?

— Nope, he saw me on the golf course.

— OK, so you got a hole-in -one on the first green.
— Now what's the bad news?

New golfer:

I want to be a golfer
in the worst way.

Caddy:

You've already made it, sir . . .

Look, you're the pro . . . tell me what to do about my game.
Well, first you should relax . . then stop playing for about six months . . . then give it up!

I got some new golf clubs for my wife.

Gee, that's great! I wish I could make a trade like that!

Darling, why don't you play golf with Harry, any more?

Would you play with a sneak who puts down the wrong score and moves his ball when you aren't looking?

Certainly not.

Well, neither will Harry!

Tell me, Reverend, is it a sin for
me to play golf on Sunday?

I've seen you on the course, my son,
and it's a sin for you to play
any day of the week.

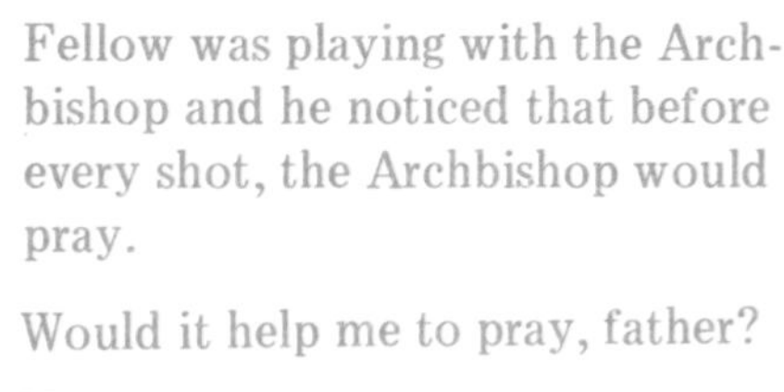

Fellow was playing with the Archbishop and he noticed that before every shot, the Archbishop would pray.

Would it help me to pray, father?

No.

Why not?

Because you're a lousy putter.

Why is it tough for ministers to play golf?

They don't have the
vocabulary for it!

What can I do to prevent topping the ball when I swing?

Try turning it upsidedown . . .

You're the Pro   How can I cut down on my strokes?

Take up painting . . .

Say, I think we should be getting closer to the club house.

What makes you think so?

We seem to be running over more golfers with the cart.

I'm sorry, sir, we have no time open on the course today.

Wait a minute, what if J. Paul Getty and Howard Hughes showed up, I'm sure you'd find a starting time for them!

Of course we would, sir.

Well, I happen to know they're not coming, so we'll take their time.

The golfer was sentenced to be hung.
Do you mind,.he said as he climbed
the scaffold, if I take a few practice swings?

Could you turn up the sound a little?

Sh-h-h-h-h, not while Arnold Palmer is putting.

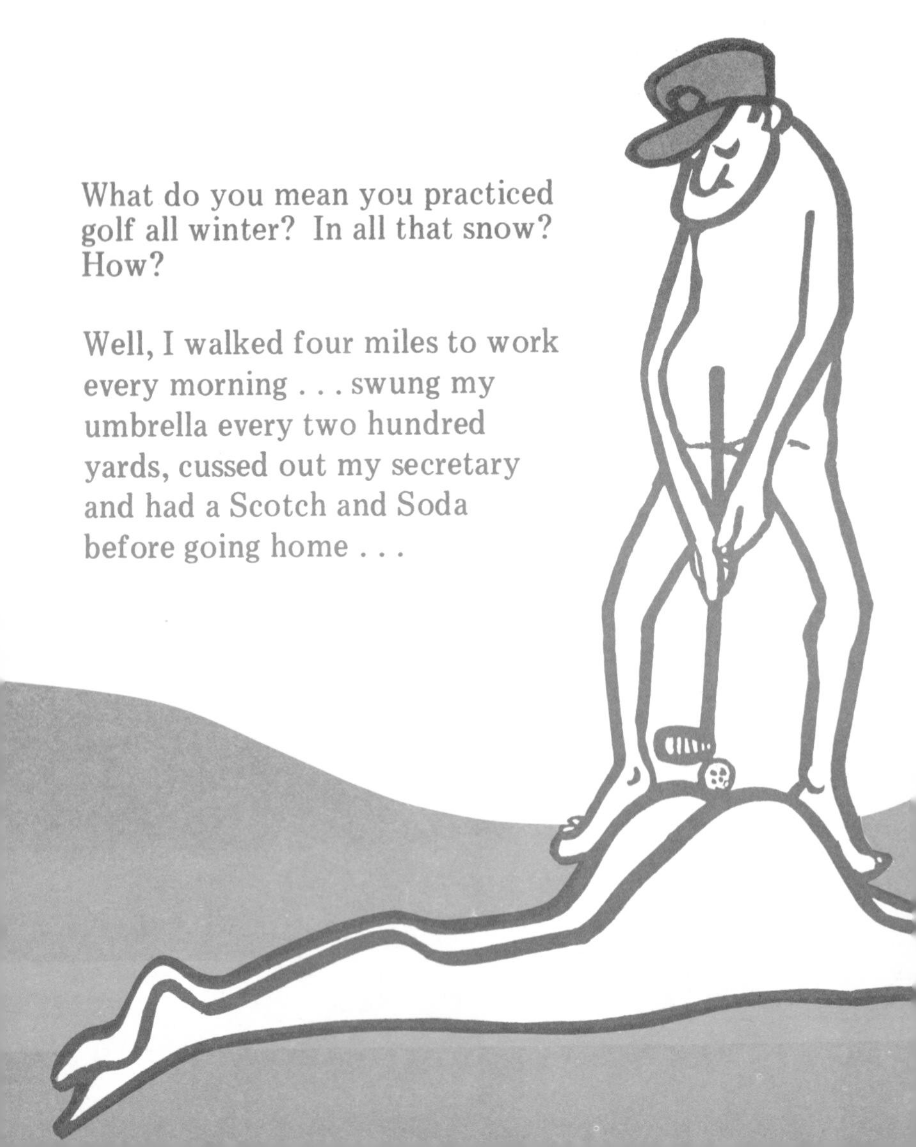
What do you mean you practiced golf all winter? In all that snow? How?
Well, I walked four miles to work every morning . . . swung my umbrella every two hundred yards, cussed out my secretary and had a Scotch and Soda before going home . . .

Wife: I know it's too much to expect, but if you ever spent a Sunday with me, instead of on the golf course, I think I'd drop dead.

Husband: It'll do no good to try and bribe me.

I don't get it, Charlie, first you slice the ball into the bushes, then across the highway, and then you lose it in the woods - and you insist on finding it?
I have to. It's my lucky ball.

That's the fourteenth time I swung at the ball and I haven't hit it.

Keep swinging . . . I think you've got it worried.

First psychiatrist missing two inch putt: Nuts!

Second psychiatrist: Come now, Harold, we agreed not to talk shop.

Doctor, the baby got into my golf bag and swallowed all my tees.

I'll be right over. What are you doing in the meantime?

I'm practicing putting.

The first time on the golf course the novice hit the ball with a mighty swing and by some miracle, it landed in the cup for a hole-in-one. On the second tee, another hole-in-one. As the ball disappeared into the hole, he turned white and trembling, and said "Gosh, I thought I missed it that time."

Golfer: Watch my swing, I don't think I'm playing my regular game.

Caddy: What game is that, sir?

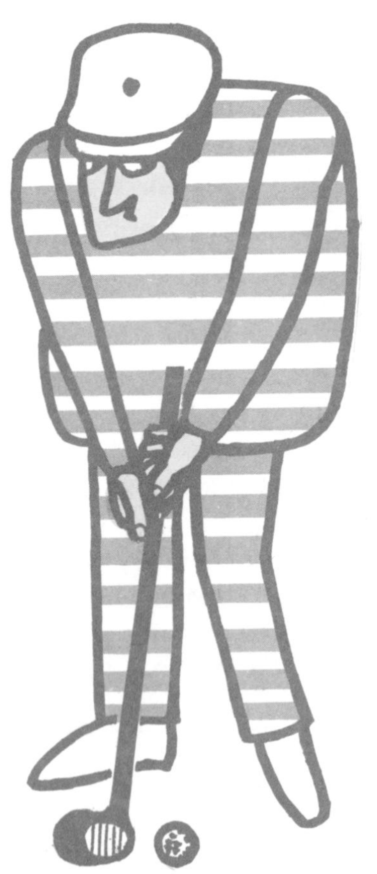

This is the first time I've played with a caddy who's only six years old . . .

You'll be crazy about him . . . he still can't count over ten.

My wife says if I don't give up golf she'll leave me.

That's terrible.

Yeah, I'm really gonna miss her.

The board fined me for hitting my wife with a number nine iron.

For conduct unbecoming a gentleman?

No, for using the wrong club.

How did you do today?

Well, I shot 9 on the first hole, 12 on the second, 16 on the third . . . but I blew it all on the fourth!

1st golfer: How come you're so late?

2nd golfer: I had to toss a coin between church and golf.

1st golfer: Then why are you so late?

2nd golfer: I had to toss seventeen times.

John, you promised to be home at 5 and now it's 9:15.

Honey, please, hear me out . . . old Charlie is dead . . . dropped dead on the 8th green.

Oh, how terrible.

It certainly was. For the rest of the day, it was hit the ball . . . drag Charlie . . . hit the ball . . . drag Charlie . . .

What's your handicap?

I'm too honest.

I've been taking golf lessons . . . spent $3,000 already.

That's a shame. You should call my brother.

Is he a golf pro?

No, he's a lawyer . . . he'll help you get your money back.

Bride: Henry, this was our wedding day. I've been waiting at the church for two hours!

Golfer: I told you, Mildred, only if it's raining. Only if it's raining.

I just hit a hole in one, yelled the golfer jubilantly.

Did you? asked his wife, who had never been on a golf course. Do it again, dear, I didn't see you.

First golfer:

It's nice of you to come to the funeral.

Second golfer:

It's the least I could do. In four more days, we would have been married thirty-six years.